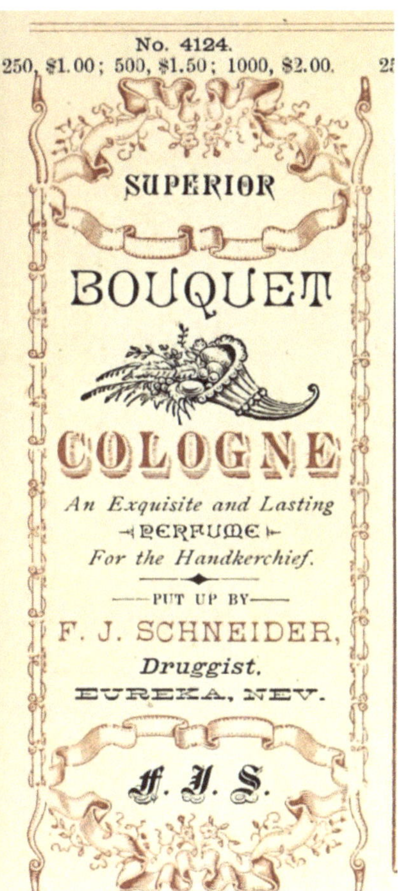

225 Vintage Red Ephemera Labels 1887

By C. Anders

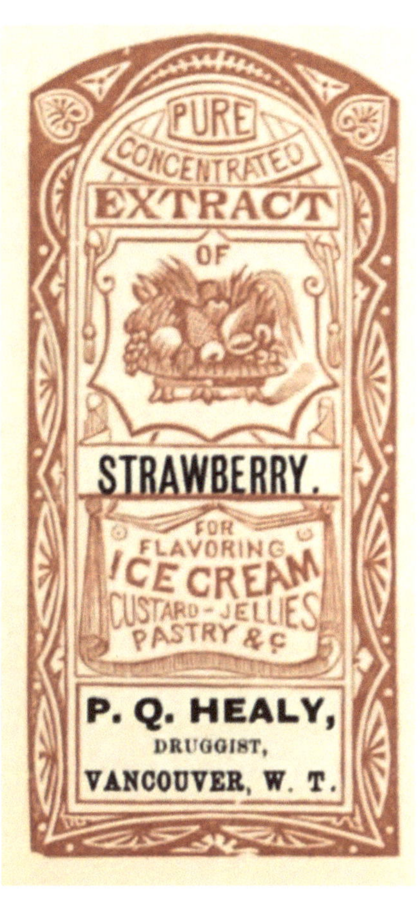

Miscellaneous Labels.

No. 3800—250, 70c; 500, 95c; 1000, $1.40.

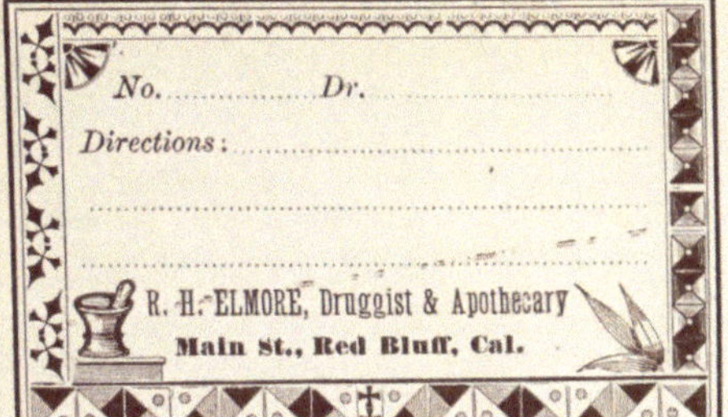

No. 3801—250, 70c; 500, 95c; 1000, $1.40.

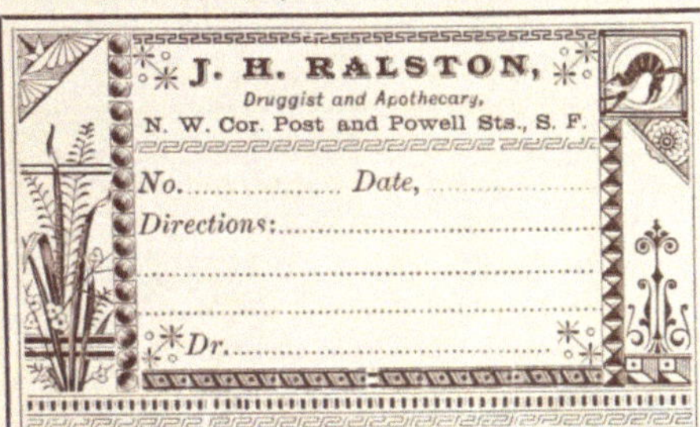

No. 3802—250, 80c; 500, $1.10; 1000, $1.60.

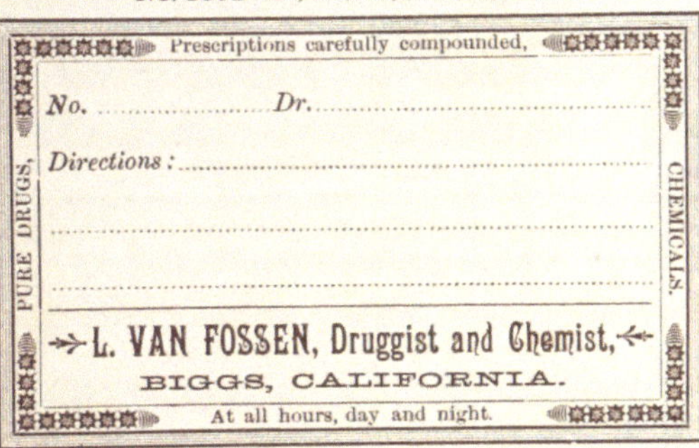

No. 3803—250, 80c; 500, $1.10; 1000, $1.60.

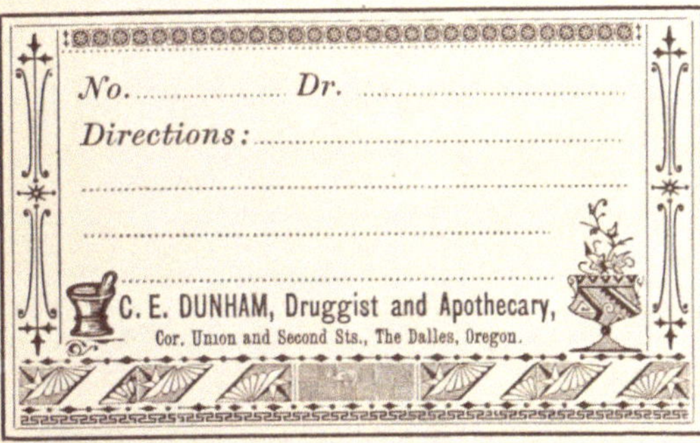

No. 3804—250, 90c; 500, $1.25; 1000, $1.80.

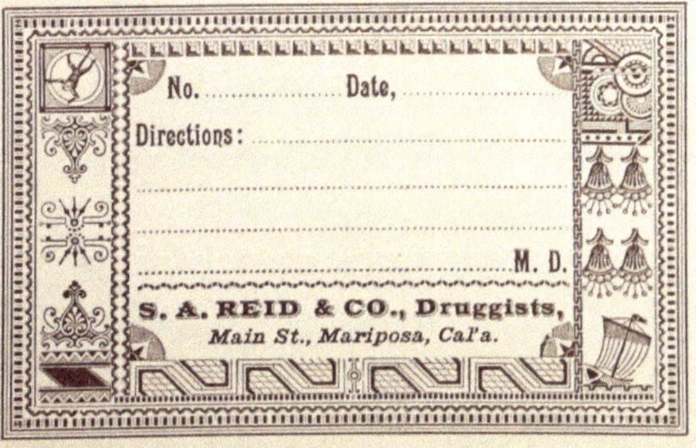

BROWN INK LABELS.

The demand for "Novelties" has induced us to add this beautiful BROWN to the list of our popular Inks. It will be found especially attractive for dispensing and toilet labels of all kinds. In fact, "a change" alone will make it acceptable for most any purpose. ALL Labels shown in Black Ink can be printed in Brown, in Green or in Lake Ink, for 20 per cent extra, on Tinted Paper for 25 per cent extra, or in two colors for 50 per cent extra, to the cost in Black Ink.

No. 3805—250, 60c; 500, 85c; 1000, $1.20.

No. 3806.   In Stock—20c per 100.

No. 3807.
In Stock—10c per 100.

No. 3808—250, $1.35; 500, $1.90; 1000, $2.75.

No. 3809—250, $1.10; 500, $1.60; 1000, $2.25.

No. 3810—250, 90c; 500, $1.25; 1000, $1.80.

All Labels shown in Brown, Green or Lake Inks, will be printed in either of the other colors at the same price, or in Black Ink for 20 per cent less.

As here shown, any Name, Dose or Poison, will be inserted, in any Label, at prices quoted. 65

No. 3846—250, 20c; 500, 30c; 1000, 40c.

No. 3847—250, 20c; 500, 30c; 1000, 40c.

No. 3848—250, 25c; 500, 35c; 1000, 50c.

No. 3849—250, 25c; 500, 35c; 1000, 50c.

No. 3850—250, 25c; 500, 35c; 1000, 50c.

No. 3851—250, 25c; 500, 35c; 1000, 50c.

No. 3852—250, 25c; 500, 35c; 1000, 50c.

No. 3853—250, 25c; 500, 35c; 1000, 50c.

LUCKEY & BRISTOW,
Dispensing Druggists,
54 WILLAMETTE ST.,
EUGENE CITY, OR.

No. 3854—250, 25c; 500, 35c; 1000, 50c.

No. 3855—250, 25c; 500, 35c; 1000, 50c.

No. 3856—250, 25c; 500, 35c; 1000, 50c.

No. 3857—250, 25c; 500, 35c; 1000, 50c.

No. 3858—250, 25c; 500, 35c; 1000, 50c.

No. 3859—250, 25c; 500, 35c; 1000, 50c.

No. 3860—250, 25c; 500, 35c; 1000, 50c.

No. 3861—250, 30c; 500, 45c; 1000, 60c.

No. 3862—250, 30c; 500, 45c; 1000, 60c.

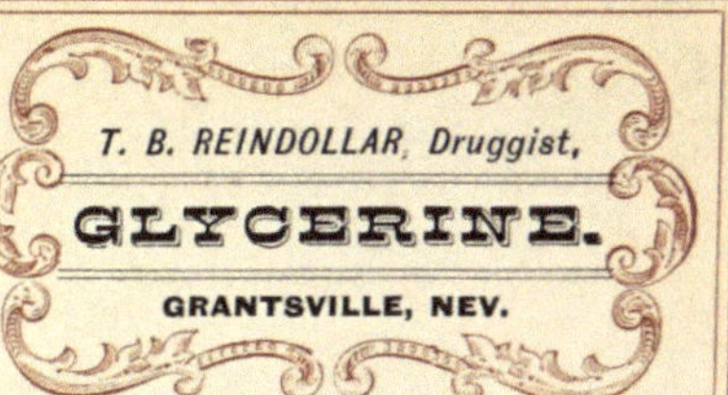

No. 3863—250, 30c; 500, 45c; 1000, 60c.

DR. J. L. EBY,
Druggist,
CREAM TARTAR.
MAIN STREET,
PETROLIA, CAL.

No. 3864—250, 30c; 500, 45c; 1000, 60c.

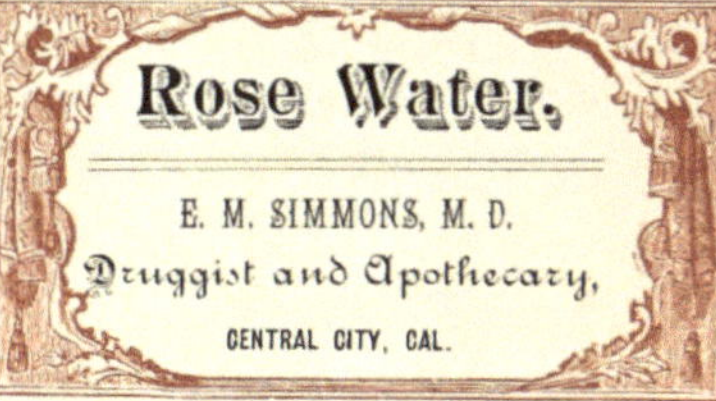

No. 3865—250, 30c; 500, 45c; 1000, 60c.

Rose Water.
E. M. SIMMONS, M. D.
Druggist and Apothecary,
CENTRAL CITY, CAL.

No. 3866—250, 30c; 500, 45c; 1000, 60c.

SPIRITS TURPENTINE.
LOUIS F. MUNROE,
Druggist and Apothecary,
Marshfield, Oregon.

No. 3867—250, 30c; 500, 45c; 1000, 60c.

No. 3868—250, 25c; 500, 35c; 1000, 50c.

W. J. HAMILTON & CO.
DRUGGISTS,
Main Street, opposite Post Office,
YAKIMA, W. T.

McNeil Bros., San Jose, Cal.

66

Pill and Toilet Labels.

No. 3869.
250, 50c; 500, 70c; 1000, $1.00.

No. 3870—250, 50c; 500, 70c; 1000, $1.00

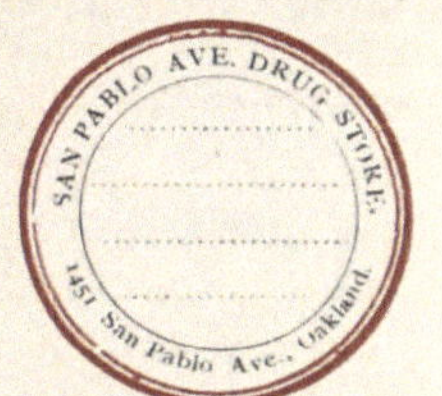

No. 3871—250, 60c; 500, 85c; 1000, $1.20

No. 3872—250, 65c; 500, 90c; 1000, $1.30.

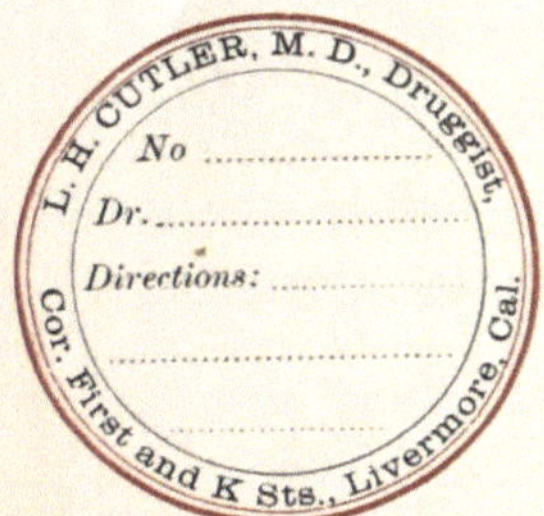

No. 3873—250, 70c; 500, 95c; 1000, $1.40.

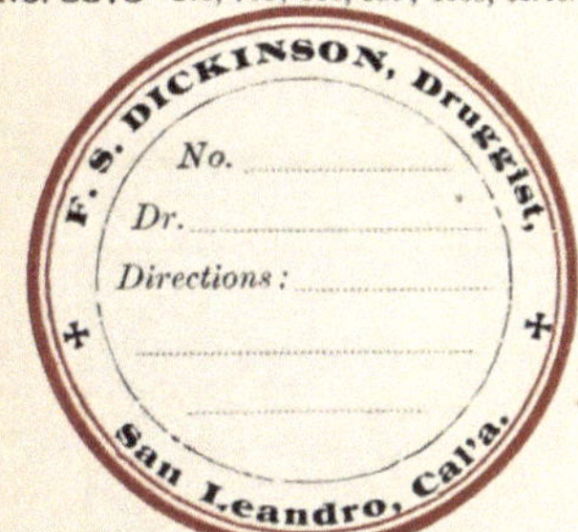

No. 3874—250, 75c; 500, $1.00; 1000, $1.50.

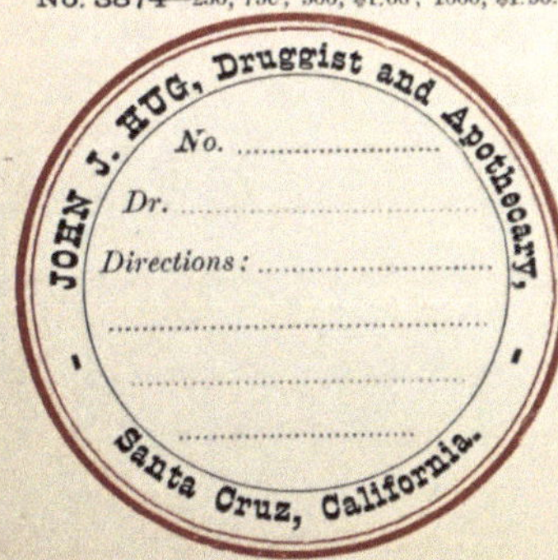

In all Dispensing Labels the words No, Dr, Date, For, Directions, Etc., can be printed, omitted or changed to suit. They can also be furnished with or without dotted lines, as desired.

No. 3875—250, 85c; 500, $1.20; $1.70.

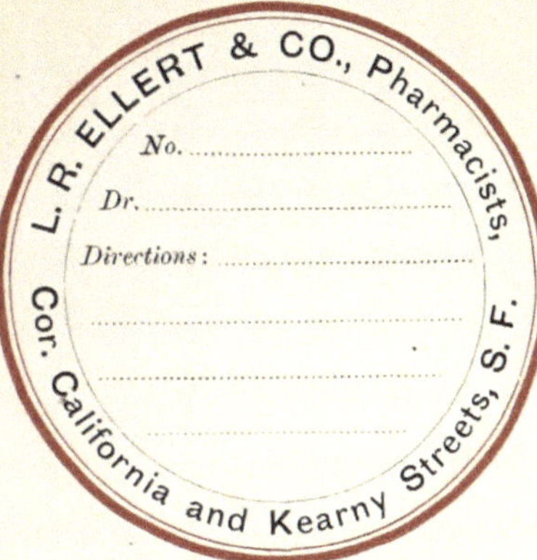

No. 3876—250, 75c; 500, $1.00; 1000, $1.40.

No. 3877—250, 85c; 500, $1.10; 1000, $1.60.

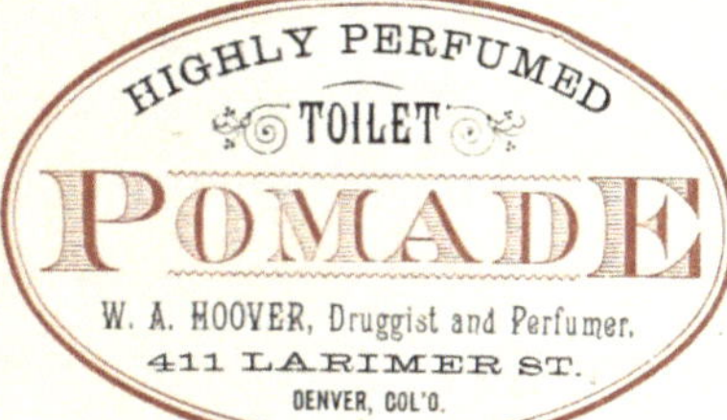

No. 3878—250, $1.10; 500, $1.50; 1000, $2.00.

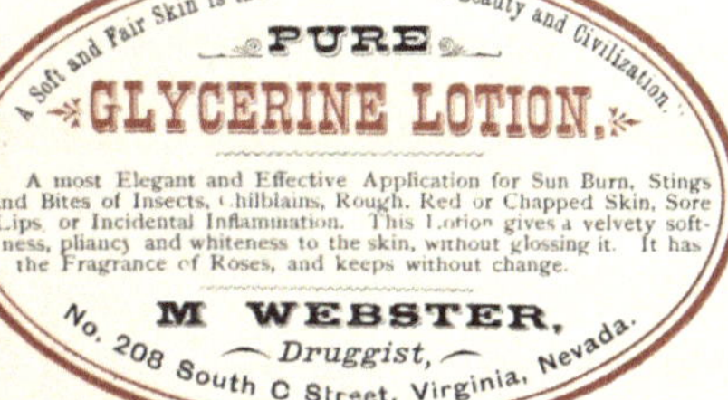

No. 3879—250, $1.25; 500, $1.75; 1000, $2.50.

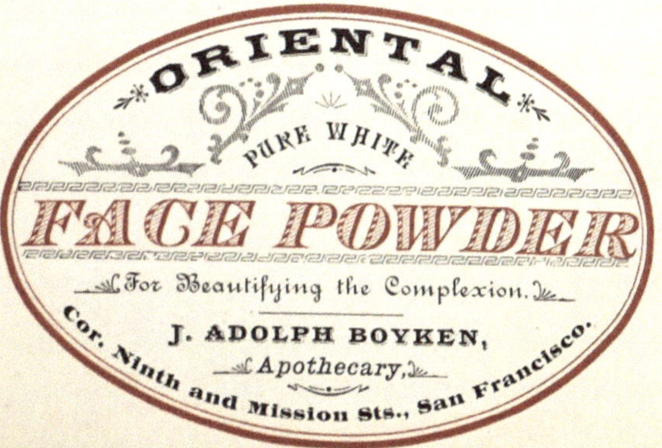

No. 3880—250, $1.25; 500, $1.75; 1000, $2.50.

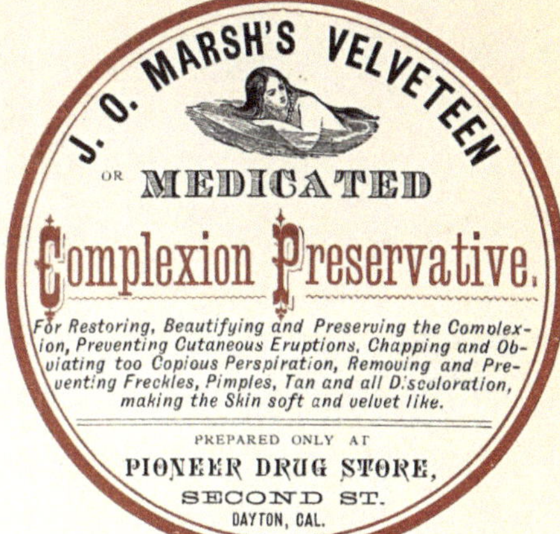

No. 3881—250, $1.10; 500, $1.50; 1000, $2.00.

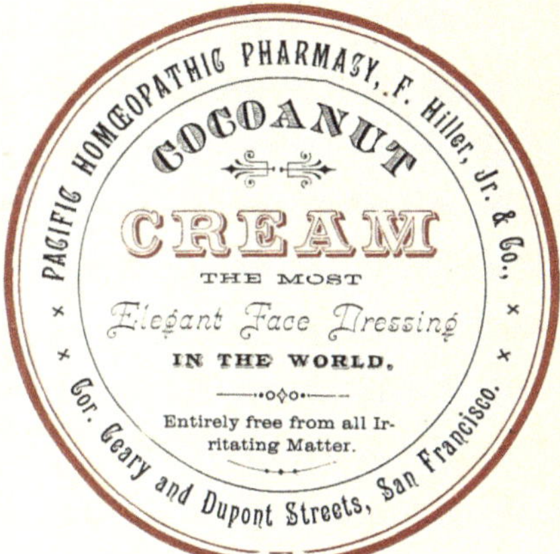

No. 3882—250, 85c; 500, $1.10; 1000, $1.60.

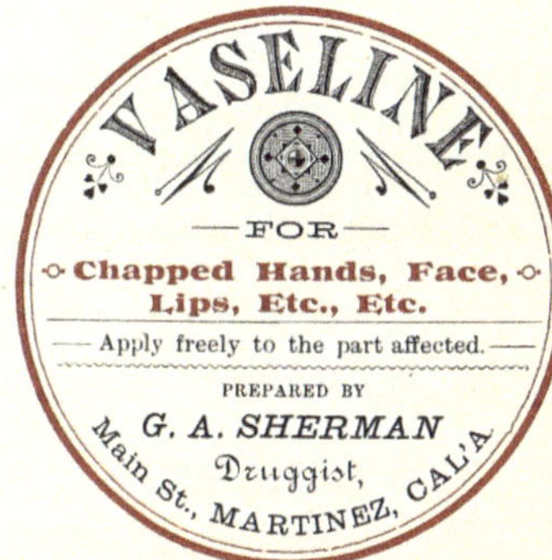

No. 3883—250, 75c; 500, $1.00; 1000, $1.50.

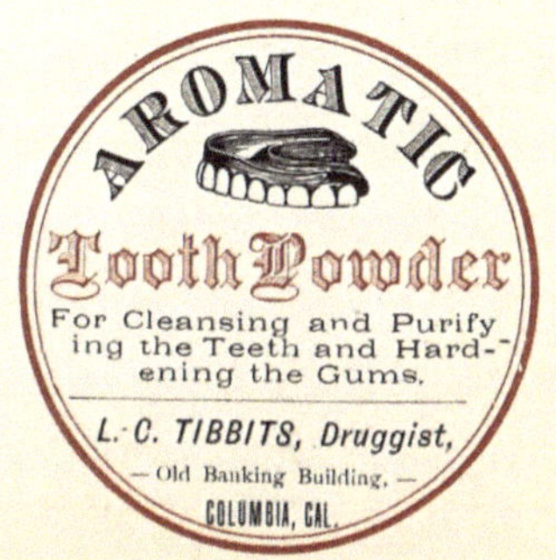

70

Dispensing Labels.

No. 3921—250, 50c ; 500, 70c ; 1000, $1.00.

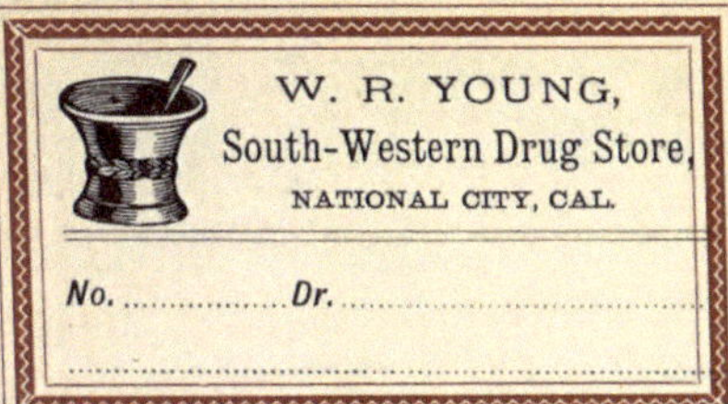

No. 3925—250, 50c ; 500, 70c ; 1000, $1 00.

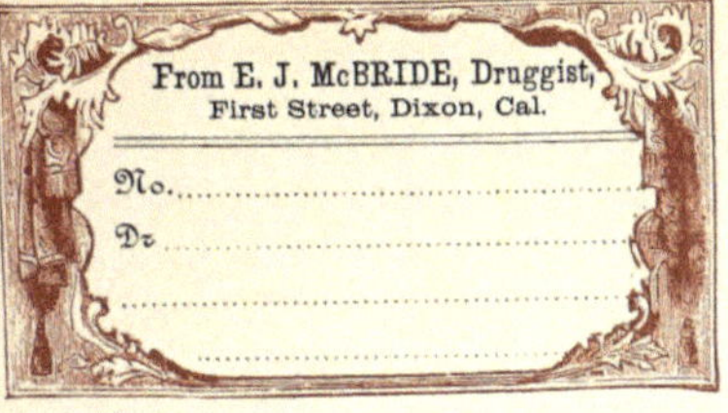

No. 3926—250, 75c ; 500, $1.00 ; 1000, $1.50.

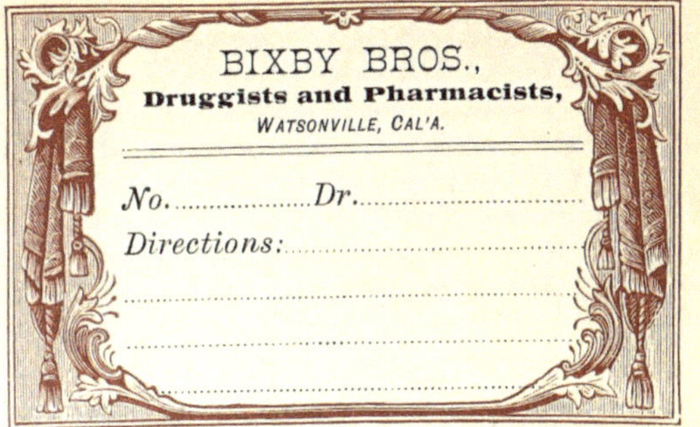

No. 3922—250, 75c ; 500, $1.00 ; 1000, $1.50.

In all Dispensing Labels the words No., Dr., Date, For, Directions, Etc., can be printed, omitted, or changed to suit. They can also be printed with or without dotted lines, as desired.

All Labels shown in Black Ink can be printed in Green, Lake or Brown Ink, for 20 per cent added to the price of Black Ink, or in two colors for 50 per cent extra.

No. 3927—250, 90c ; 500, $1.25 ; 1000, $1.80.

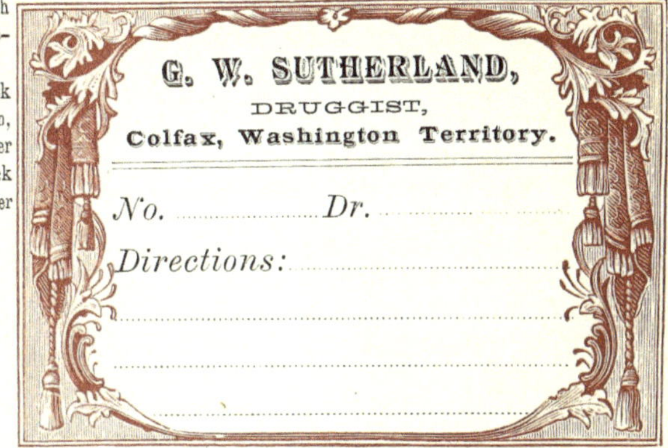

No. 3923—250, 90c ; 500, $1.25 ; 1000, $1.80.

No. 3928—250, 50c ; 500, 70c ; 1000, $1.00.

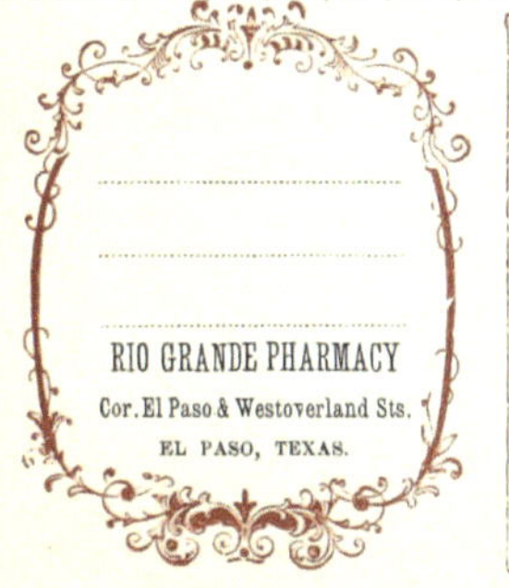

No. 3929—250, 75c ; 500, $1.00 ; 1000, $1.50.

No. 3924—250, $1.10 ; 500, $1.60 ; 1000, $2.25.

No. 3930—250, $1.25 ; 500, $1.75 ; 1000, $2.50.

McNeil Bros., San Jose, Cal.

No. 3957.
250, 90c; 500, $1.25; 1000, $1.80.

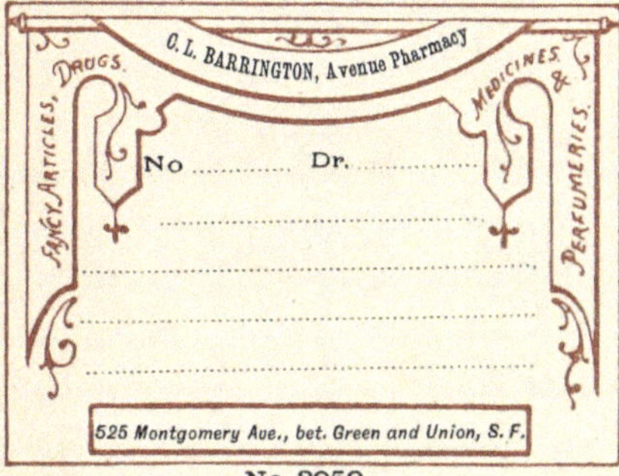

No. 3958.
250, 75c; 500, $1.00; 1000, $1.50.

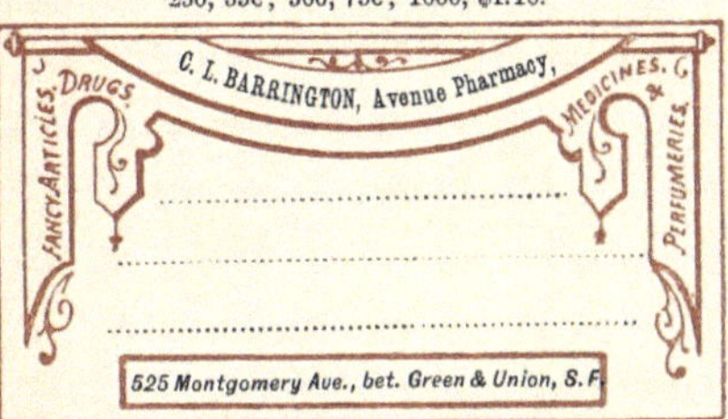

No. 3959.
250, 55c; 500, 75c; 1000, $1.10.

No. 3960.
250, 75c; 500, $1.10; 1000, $1.50.

No.
Dr.
Directions:

BOERICKE & TAFEL,
Druggists,
956 Broadway, Oakland, Cal.

In all Dispensing Labels the words No., Dr., For, Date, Directions, Etc., can be printed, omitted, or changed to suit.   They can also be printed with or without dotted lines, as desired.

All Labels shown in Black Ink can be printed in Green, Lake, or Brown Ink, for 20 per cent. added to the price of Black Ink, or in two colors for fifty per cent extra.

No. 3962.
250, 70c; 500, 95c; 1000, $1.40.

GARDEN CITY DRUG STORE,
Washington St.,
PHŒNIX, - ARIZONA.

No.
Date,
Dr.
Directions:

No. 3963.
250, 60c; 500, 85c; 1000, $1.20.

No. 3964.
250, 75c; 500, $1.10; 1000, $1.50.

No.

J. W. RULE, Apothecary,
Cor. Third and Howard Sts.,
—S. F.—

No. 3965—250, 65c; 500, 90c; 1000, $1.30.

LINIMENT.

E. J. McBRIDE, Druggist and Bookseller,
DIXON, - CAL'A.

No. 3966—250, 90c; 500, $1.25; 1000, $1.80.

GEO. WAPPLE.
DRUGGIST,
San Benito Street, - Hollister, Cal.

No.   Dr.
Directions:

No. 3967—250, 80c; 500, $1.10; 1000, $1.60.

H. S. DANIELS & SON,
DRUGGISTS,
Crawford Street, Downey City, Cal.

No.   Dr.
Directions:

No. 3968—250, 70c; 500, 95c; 1000, $1.40.

H. S. DANIELS & SON,
DRUGGISTS,
Crawford St., Downey City, Cal.

No.   Date
Directions:

No. 3969—250, 55c; 500, 75c; 1000, $1.10.

H. S. DANIELS & SON,
DRUGGISTS,
Crawford St., Downey City, Cal.

No.   Dr.
Directions:

No. 3961.
250, 60c; 500, 85c; 1000, $1.20.

BOERICKE & TAFEL,
DRUGGISTS,
956 Broadway, Oakland, Cal.

No. 3970.
250, 60c; 500, 85c; 1000, $1.20.

C. F. NIECE,
DRUGGIST,
118 Main Street,
LOS ANGELES, CAL.

No.

No. 3971—250, $1.50; 500, $2.00; 1000, $3.00.

No. 3972—250, $1.10; 500, $1.60; 1000, $2.25.

EFFERVESCING SOLUTION
:—OF:—
CITRATE OF MAGNESIA,
OR PURGATIVE LEMONADE.

This Refrigerant and Laxative Preparation is well known as an agreeable substitute for Epsom Salts, Seidlitz Powders, and the Saline Cathartics generally.

THE contents of this bottle is a full purgative dose. For children, from a teaspoonful to a wine-glassful may be given, and repeated if required. The bottle should be kept corked in the intervals of taking.

From JOHN WOLFE, Druggist,
SAN RAFAEL, CAL.

No. 3973—250, $1.10; 500, $1.60; 1000, $2.25.

EFFERVESCING SOLUTION
—OF—
CITRATE OF MAGNESIA,
OR PURGATIVE LEMONADE.

This Refrigerant and Laxative Preparation is well known as an agreeable substitute for Epsom Salts, Seidlitz Powders, and the Saline Cathartics generally.

The contents of this bottle is a full purgative dose. For Children, from a tea-spoonful to a wine-glassful may be given, and repeated if required. The bottle should be kept corked in the intervals of taking.

PREPARED BY
W. B. PIXLEY, Apothecary,
N. E. Cor. Stockton and O'Farrell Sts., San Francisco.

No. 3974—250, $1.35; 500, $1.90; 1000, $2.75.

IMPROVED EFFERVESCING SOLUTION
CITRATE of MAGNESIA
OR LEMON PURGATIVE.

DIRECTIONS FOR USE.

FOR CATHARTIC—The contents of the bottle may be taken at one dose in the morning.

FOR LAXATIVE—A wine-glassful every two hours until the desired effect is produced; or half the contents of the bottle may be taken at once, and the remainder in an hour or two if it does not operate.

FOR REFRIGERANT—A tablespoonful every hour or two.

☞ Keep the bottle in a cool place, with the cork down.

PREPARED AT

Watsonville Drug Store, - G. A. MOREHEAD, Proprietor,
Main Street, Watsonville, Cal.

No. 3975—250, $1.25; 500, $1.75; 1000, $2.50.

SOLUTION OF
CITRATE ✧ OF ✧ MAGNESIA,
OR PURGATIVE MINERAL WATER.

This valuable preparation is well known as an agreeable substitute for Epsom Salts, Seidlitz Powders, and Saline Cathartics generally.

DIRECTIONS.—As a Refrigerant, a tablespoonful every hour or two. As a Laxative, a wine-glassful as often until the desired effect is induced. As a Purgative, half the contents of a bottle may be taken at once, and the remaining half in an hour or two if it does not operate. The bottle should be kept well corked in the intervals of taking.

✧ E. F. LIEBRICH, Pharmacist, ✧
Cor. Eddy and Steiner Streets, San Francisco.

No. 3976.
250, $1.00; 500, $1.40; 1000, $2.00.

EFFERVESCING SOLUTION
—OF—
CITRATE
—OF—
MAGNESIA
—OR—
Purgative Mineral Water.

This refrigerant and laxative preparation is well known as an agreeable substitute for Epsom Salts, Seidlitz Powders, and the Saline Cathartics generally.

The contents of one bottle is a full purgative dose. For children, from a tablespoonful to a wine-glassful may be given, and repeated if desired. The bottle should be kept corked in the intervals of taking.

PREPARED BY

JOHN R. WILLIAMS,
220 MAIN ST.,
STOCKTON, CAL.

No. 3977—250, $1.25; 500, $1.75; 1000, $2.50.

EFFERVESCING SOLUTION
OF
CITRATE of MAGNESIA
OR
PURGATIVE MINERAL WATER.

This Refrigerant and Laxative Preparation is well known as an agreeable substitute for Epsom Salts, Seidlitz Powders, and the Saline Cathartics generally.

THE contents of this bottle is a full purgative dose. For children, from a teaspoonful to a wine-glassful may be given, and repeated if required. The bottle should be kept corked in the intervals of taking.

PREPARED AT
CORNER DRUG STORE,
Corner Geary and Buchanan Sts.,
SAN FRANCISCO.

McNeil Bros., San Jose, Cal.

Castor Oil Labels.

No. 3994—250, $1.35; 500, $1.90; 1000, $2.75.

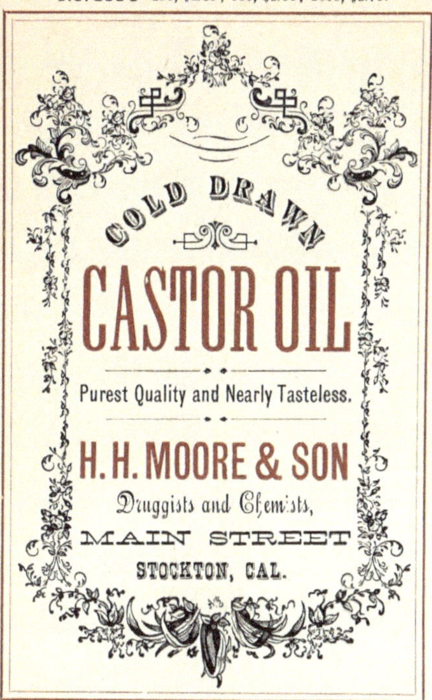

No. 3995—250, $1.25; 500, $1.75; 1000, $2.50.

No. 3996.
250, $1.00; 500, $1.50; 1000, $2.00.

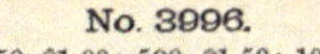

No. 3997.
250, 80c; 500, $1.10; 1000, $1.60.

No. 3998—250, $1.25; 500, $1.75; 1000, $2.50.

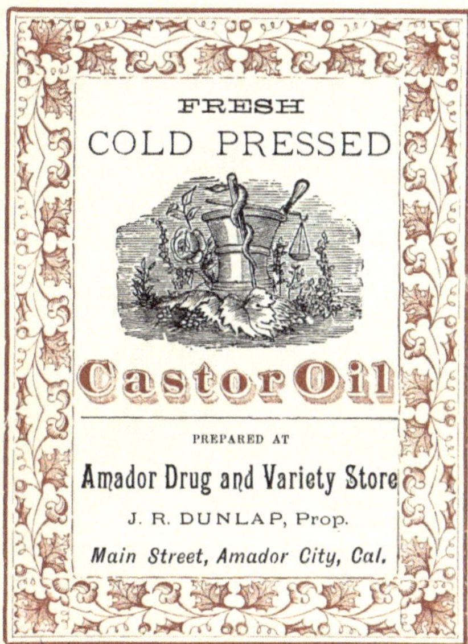

No. 3999—250, $1.00; 500, $1.40; 1000, $2.00.

No. 4000.
250, 65c; 500, 90c; 1000, $1.30.

No. 4001.
250, 80c; 500, $1.10; 1000, $1.60.

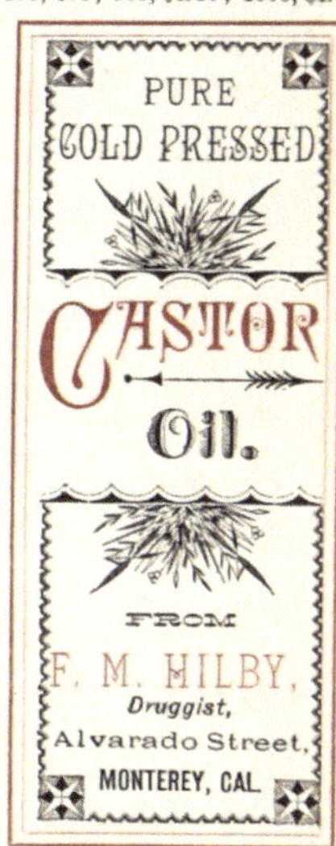

No. 4002—250, $1.00; 500, $1.40; 1000, $2.00.

No. 4003—250, $1.00; 500, $1.40; 1000, $2.00.

No. 4004—250, $1.00; 500, $1.40; 1000, $2.00.

80

Cough and Lung Syrup Labels.

No. 4025.
250, $1.00; 500, $1.40; 1000, $2.00.

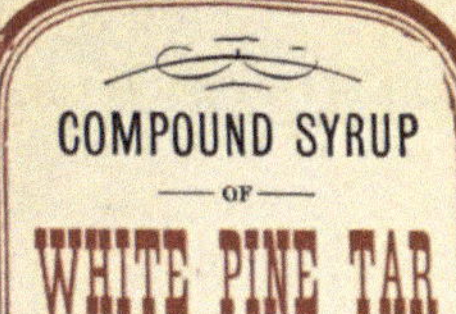

COMPOUND SYRUP
OF
WHITE PINE TAR
AND
WILD CHERRY,
An Invaluable Remedy for the Cure of
COUGHS, COLDS,
BRONCHITIS,
And Other Diseases of the
THROAT AND LUNGS.

DOSE.—For adults, a teaspoonful whenever Cough is troublesome. For children, less, in proportion to age.

PREPARED BY
THEO. RUTH,
Druggist,
POMONA, CAL.

No. 4026.
250, $1.10; 500, $1.60; 1000, $2.25.

WILD CHERRY
COUGH
BALSAM
AND
CORDIAL.
A CURE FOR
Coughs, Colds, Affections of the Throat, Diseases of the Lungs, Chest Complaints, Etc.

DOSE.—Adults, one teaspoonful every three hours. Children, the dose should be graduated according to age.

PREPARED BY
W. E. McCARTNEY & BRO.
Dispensing Chemists,
YALE, B. C.

No. 4027.
250, $1.10; 500, $1.50; 1000, $2.00.

Dr. MOTT'S
CELEBRATED
FAMILY
Cough Syrup
A Safe, Pleasant and Efficient Remedy for
Coughs, Colds, Asthma, Bronchitis, Sore Throat, Hoarseness, and all Affections of the
THROAT AND LUNGS.

DIRECTIONS.

For an adult, 2 teaspoonfuls; 10 years old, 1 teaspoonful; 4 years old, ½ teaspoonful; 1 to 2 years old, 10 to 15 drops, three or four times a day.

PREPARED AT THE
SOUTH END PHARMACY,
501 6th Street,
SAN FRANCISCO.

No. 4028.
250, $1.00; 500, $1.50; 1000, $2.00.

DR. MURPHY'S
PECTORAL
COUGH
SYRUP,
A Valuable Remedy for
COUGHS, COLDS,
Sore Throat, Bronchitis,
And all Diseases of the
THROAT AND LUNGS

DIRECTIONS.—For an Adult 1 teaspoonful every 1, 2 or 3 hours, as the case may require. Proportionately less for children.

PREPARED BY
L. D. MURPHY, M. D.
Physician and Surgeon,
TULARE CITY, CAL.

No. 4029.
250, 75c; 500, $1.00; 1000, $1.50.

PULMONARY
COUGH
Syrup.
A Valuable Remedy for
Coughs, Colds, Sore Throat, Bronchitis, and all Diseases of the
THROAT AND LUNGS.

DIRECTIONS.—For an adult, 1 teaspoonful every 1, 2, or 3 hours, as the case may require. Proportionately less for children.

PREPARED BY
C. E. DUNHAM, Druggist,
THE DALLES, OR.

No. 4030—250, $1.10; 500, $1.60; 1000, $2.25.

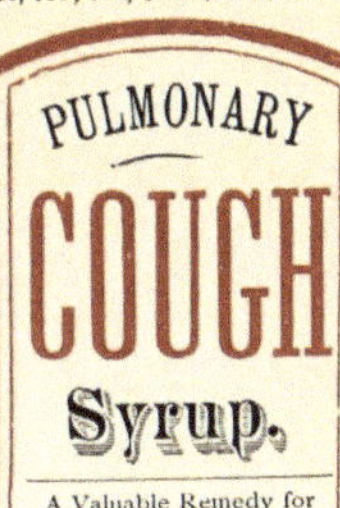

COMPOUND
Cough Syrup
FOR
Coughs, Colds, Bronchitis, Sore Throat, Hoarseness,
AND ALL
DISEASES OF THE THROAT AND LUNGS.

DIRECTIONS.—Ordinary or medium dose, one teaspoonful every 3 or 4 hours. For Hoarseness or Sore Throat, use in small quantities and take often. For children, give according to age.

PREPARED BY
R. B. TILGHMAN & CO.,
—Druggists,—
Next to T. W. Miller's, 2d St., The Dalles, Or.

No. 4031—250, 60c; 500, 95c; 1000, $1.40.

COMPOUND
COUGH SYRUP,
FOR THE CURE OF
Coughs, Colds, Hoarseness, Sore Throat, Bronchitis, and all Diseases of the Throat and Lungs.

Directions.—For a grown person, a teaspoonful; 15 to 20 years, ½ teaspoonful, four times during the day, and double the dose at bed time.

PREPARED AND SOLD BY
W. E. FIFIELD, Druggist
Madison, Cal.

No. 4032.
250, 65c; 500, 90c; 1000, $1.30.

MANN'S
COMPOUND
HONEY
SYRUP,
—:FOR:—
Coughs, Colds, Hoarseness, Bronchitis, Sore Throat, Croup, Etc.

DOSE.—Adults, one teaspoonful; Children five to fifteen drops.

C. B. MANN,
PHARMACIST,
OLYMPIA, W. T.

No. 4033.
250, $1.25; 500, $1.75; 1000, $2.50.

INDIAN
Throat & Lung
SYRUP.
Superior to all Lung and Throat Remedies now before the Public
FOR THE CURE OF
Coughs, Colds, Croup, Whooping Cough, Sore Throat, Difficulty of Breathing, Asthma, Etc.

DOSE.—For Adults, a teaspoonful. For children, from 15 to 20 drops, according to age. To be taken before meals and on going to bed.

PREPARED AT
PARRISH'S PHARMACY,
269 First St.,
PORTLAND, OR.

No. 4034—250, 80c; 500, $1.10; 1000, $1.60.

COMPOUND
COUGH SYRUP
Valuable for the Relief of Coughs, Colds, Hoarseness, Sore Throat, Bronchitis, and all Diseases of the Throat and Lungs.

Directions.—For an adult, a teaspoonful; Children, in proportion to age. To be taken when the Cough is troublesome.

Prepared by THOMPSON & CO., Chemists,
Kohala, Hawaiian Islands.

No. 4035.
250, 65c; 500, 90c; 1000, $1.30.

WILD CHERRY
COUGH BALSAM
FOR
COUGHS, COLDS, CROUP, SORE THROAT, HOARSENESS, ETC.

DOSE.—Adults, one teaspoonful three times a day. Children, according to age.

J. G. BOOTH,
Druggist and Apothecary,
TRUCKEE, CAL.

No. 4036—250, 65c; 500, 90c; 1000, $1.30.

SUPERIOR
COUGH MIXTURE
A SPEEDY AND SURE CURE FOR
COUGHS, COLDS, CROUP, HOARSENESS, ETC.

J. M. KITCHEN, DRUGGIST,
Irving, Oregon.

McNeil Bros., San Jose, Cal.

Miscellaneous Labels.

No. 4073.
250, 95c ; 500, $1.25 ; 1000, $1.80.

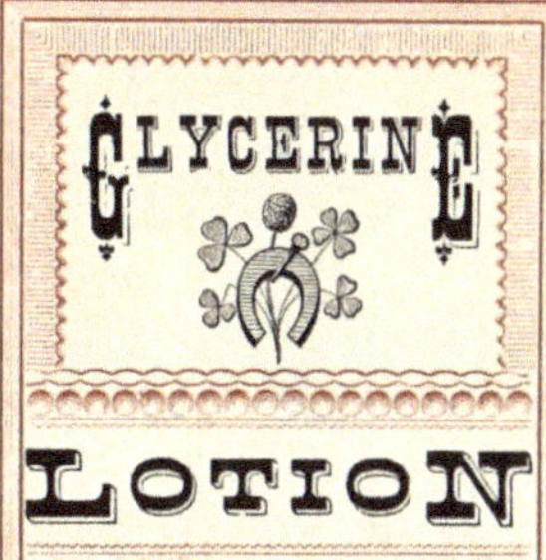

No. 4074.
250, $1.00 ; 500, $1.40 ; 1000, $2.00.

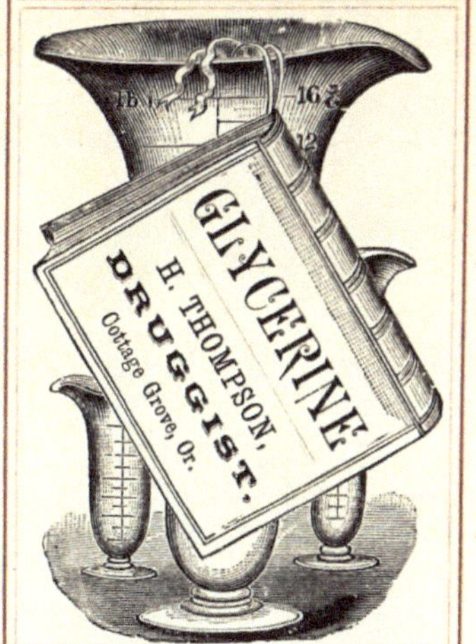

No. 4075.
250, 70c ; 500, 95c ; 1000, $1.40.

No. 4076.
250, $1.35 ; 500, $1.90 ; 1000, $2.75.

No. 4077.
250, 75c ; 500, $1.00 ; 1000, $1.50.

No. 4078.
250, 70c ; 500, 95c ; 1000, $1.40.

No. 4079.
250, 80c ; 500, $1.10 ; 1000, $1.60.

No. 4080—250, 80c ; 500, $1.10 ; 1000, $1.60.

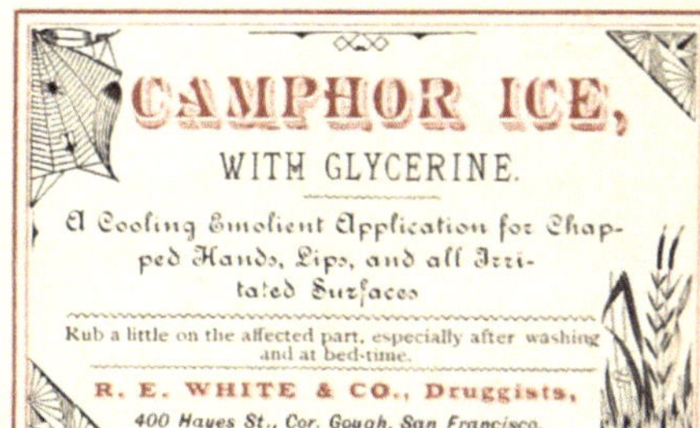

No. 4081.
250, 90c ; 500, $1.25 ; 1000, $1.80.

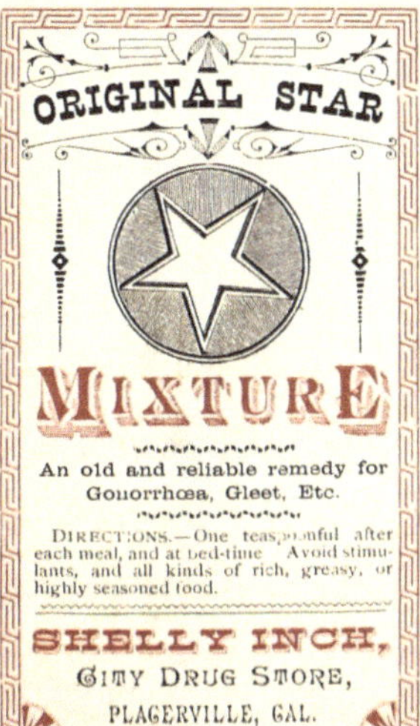

No. 4082.
250, $1.25 ; 500, $1.75 ; 1000, $2.50.

No. 4083.
250, $1.10 ; 500, $1.60 ; 1000, $2.25.

No. 4084.
250, $1.10 ; 500, $1.60 ; 1000, $2.25.

86   *Flavoring Extract Labels.*

In all Flavoring Extracts, the Name of Article can be changed without extra charge.

No. 4085.	No. 4086.	No. 4087.	No. 4088.	No. 4089.
250, $1.25; 500, $1.75; 1000, $2.50.	250, $1.25; 500, $1.75; 1000, $2.50.	250, $1.25; 500, $1.75; 1000, $2.50.	250, $1.25; 500, $1.75; 1000, $2.50.	250, $1.25; 500, $1.75; 1000, $2.50.

No. 4090.	No. 4091.	No. 4092.	No. 4093.	No. 4094.	No. 4095.

Nos. 4090 to 4095—250, 75c; 500, $1.00; 1000, $1.50.

No. 4090.

PURE
CONCENTRATED
ESSENCE
:OF:
PEPPERMINT
FOR FLAVORING
Ice Cream, Custards,
Pastry, Jellies, Etc.
Use to Suit the Taste.
WATSON BROS.,
Druggists,
ELLENSBURG, W. T.

No. 4091.

KOHLMAN'S
PURE
CONCENTRATED
EXTRACT
OF
ORANGE
FOR
Flavoring Ice Cream,
Custards, Jellies,
Pastry, Etc.
USE TO SUIT THE TASTE
S. KOHLMAN, Grocer,
216 Sixth Street,
Bet. Howard & Folsom, S. F.

No. 4092.

PURE
CONCENTRATED
EXTRACT
:OF:
ALMOND
For Flavoring
ICE CREAM,
Jellies,
CUSTARDS,
Pastry, Etc.
C. NEUMANN,
Cheap Cash Grocer,
1307 Polk St.,
SAN FRANCISCO, CAL.

No. 4093.

PURE
CONCENTRATED
EXTRACT
—OF—
PINEAPPLE
For Flavoring Ice Cream,
Custards, Jellies,
Pastry, Etc.
Use to Suit the Taste.
PREPARED BY
J. MOURON
Druggist,
SONORA, CAL.

No. 4094.

SUPERIOR
EXTRACT
—:OF:—
VANILLA
For Flavoring Ice Cream,
Custards. Jellies,
Pastry, Etc.
KIRK, CEARY & CO.
Wholesale and Retail
DRUGGISTS,
416 J Street,
SACRAMENTO, CAL.

No. 4095.

PURE
CONCENTRATED
EXTRACT
—:OF:—
LEMON
For Flavoring
Ice Cream, Jellies
Pastry, Etc.
JOS. PALMER
City Drug Store,
LA GRANDE, OR'N.

No. 4096.	No. 4097.	No. 4098.	No. 4099.	No. 4100.	No. 4101.

Nos. 4096 to 4101—250, 75c; 500, $1.00; 1000, $1.50.

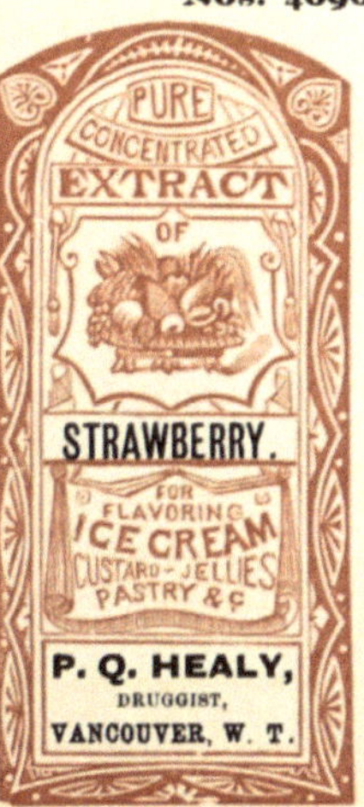

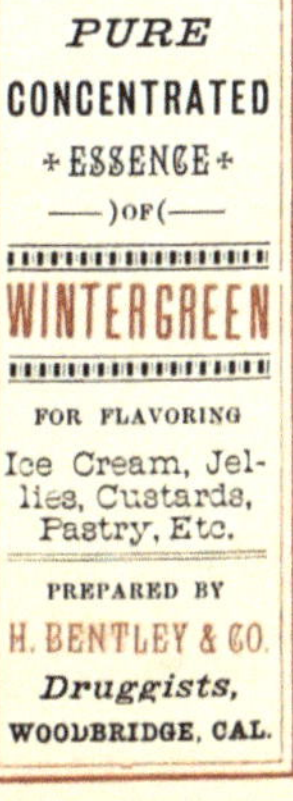

PURE
CONCENTRATED
ESSENCE
)OF(
WINTERGREEN
FOR FLAVORING
Ice Cream, Jel-
lies, Custards,
Pastry, Etc.
PREPARED BY
H. BENTLEY & CO.
Druggists,
WOODBRIDGE, CAL.

Miscellaneous Labels.

In all Flavoring Extracts, the Name of Article can be changed without extra charge.

No. 4102.
250, $1.35; 500, $1.90; 1000, $2.75.

No. 4103.
250, $1.50; 500, $2.00; 1000, $3.00.

No. 4104.
250, $1.60; 500, $2.20; 1000, $3.25.

No. 4105.
250, $1.75; 500, $2.35; 1000, $3.50.

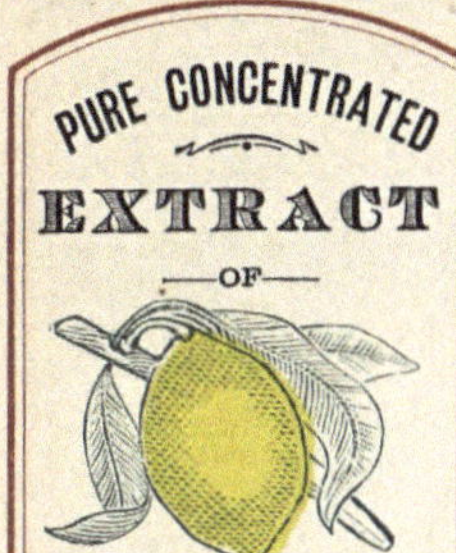

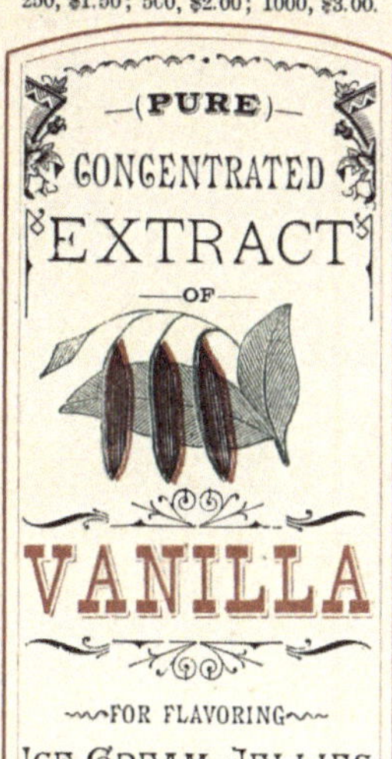

No. 4106.
250, 45c; 500, 65c; 1000, 90c.

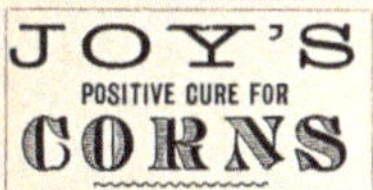

No. 4107.
250, 40c; 500, 60c; 1000, 80c.

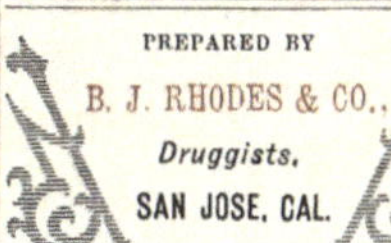

No. 4108.
250, 35c; 500, 50c; 1000, 70c.

Owing to the method of manufacturing the above Flavoring Extract Labels, Nos. 4102 to 4105 will NOT be gummed. We do not print less than 250 to each name.

No. 4109.
250, 80c; 500, $1.10; 1000, $1.60.

No. 4110.
250, 80c; 500, $1.10; 1000, $1.60.

No. 4111.
250, $1.00; 500, $1.40; 1000, $2.00.

No. 4112.
250, 80c; 500, $1.10; 1000, $1.60.

No. 4113.
250, 90c; 500, $1.25; 1000, $1.80.

McNeil Bros., San Jose, Cal.

Toilet Labels.

IN ALL TOILET LABELS THE NAME OF ARTICLE WILL BE CHANGED WITHOUT EXTRA CHARGE.

No. 4114—250, $1.25; 500, $1.75; 1000, $2.50.

No. 4115—250, $1.25; 500, $1.75; 1000, $2.50.

No. 4116—250, $1.25; 500, $1.75; 1000, $2.50.

No. 4117—250, $1.25; 500, $1.75; 1000, $2.50.

No. 4118—250, $1.25; 500, $1.75; 1000, $2.50.

No. 4119—250, $1.25; 500, $1.75; 1000, $2.50.

SUPERIOR

JOCKEY CLUB,

FOR THE TOILET.

C. H. DARROUGH,

Druggist and Pharmacist

OPPOSITE TREMONT BLOCK

RED BLUFF, CAL.

No. 4120.
250, 35c; 500, 50c; 1000, 70c.

No. 4121.
250, 70c; 500, 95c; 1000, $1.40.

No. 4122.
250, 70c; 500, 95c; 1000, $1.40.

No. 4123.
250, 75c; 500, $1.00; 1000, $1.50.

EDWIN JOY & CO.,
Druggists and Perfumers,

NEW MOWN HAY.

852 Market Street,
SAN FRANCISCO.

TAKE NOTICE.

No. 4120 is also furnished, *in lots of 1000 or over* ONLY, at 20 cents for each 125, the name of article being changed for every 125 Labels. By this means, Druggists can obtain a variety of Perfumery Labels at a nominal cost. For list of perfumeries, see page 48.

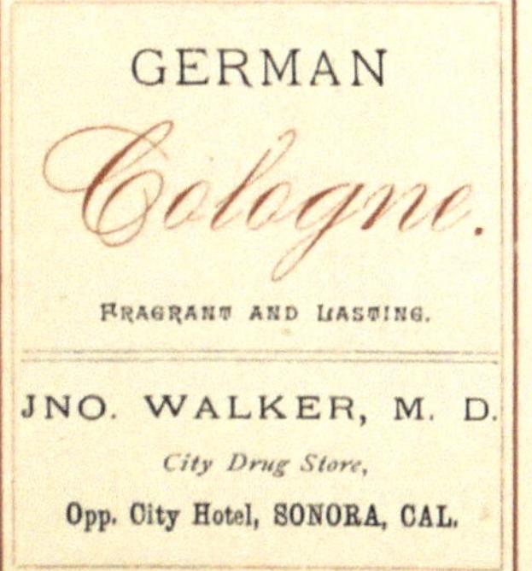

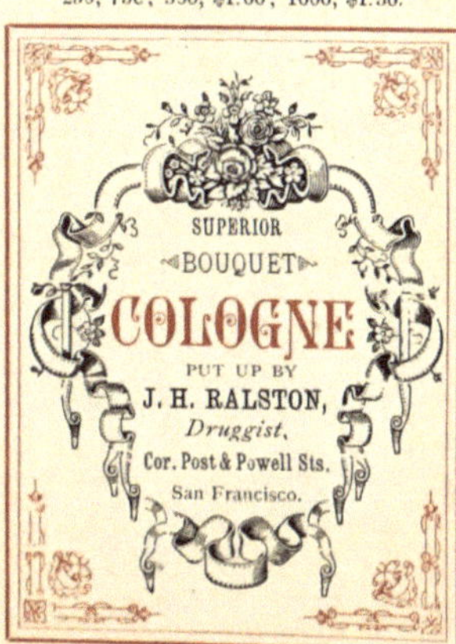

Except when expressly so stated, we do not furnish less than 250 Labels to any one name of article.

McNeil Bros., San Jose, Cal.

Toilet Labels.

No. 4124.
250, $1.00; 500, $1.50; 1000, $2.00.

No. 4125.
250, 90c; 500 $1.25; 1000, $1.80.

No. 4126.
250, 90c; 500, $1.25; 1000, $1.80.

No. 4127—250, $1.35; 500, $1.90; 1000, $2.75.

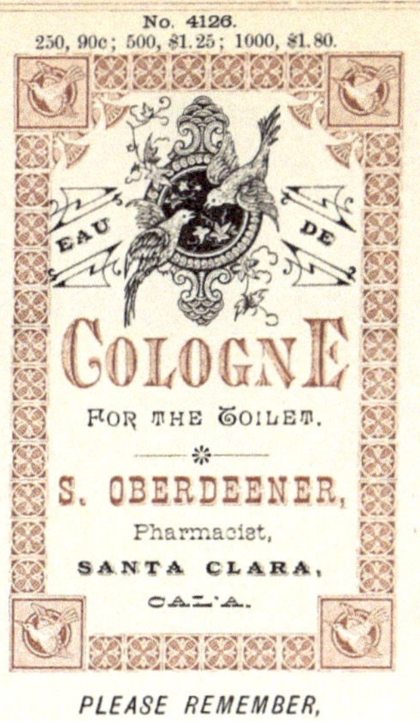

PLEASE REMEMBER,

That unless it is expressly so stated, and price per 100 quoted over each Label, we do not furnish less than 250 to each name of article.

No. 4128—250, 90c; 500, $1.25; 1000, $1.80.

No. 4129—250, $1.25; 500, $1.75; 1000, $2.50.

No. 4130—250, $1.25; 500, $1.75; 1000, $2.50.

No. 4131—250, 90c; 500, $1.25; 1000, $1.80.

No. 4134.
250, 80c; 500, $1.10; 1000, $1.60.

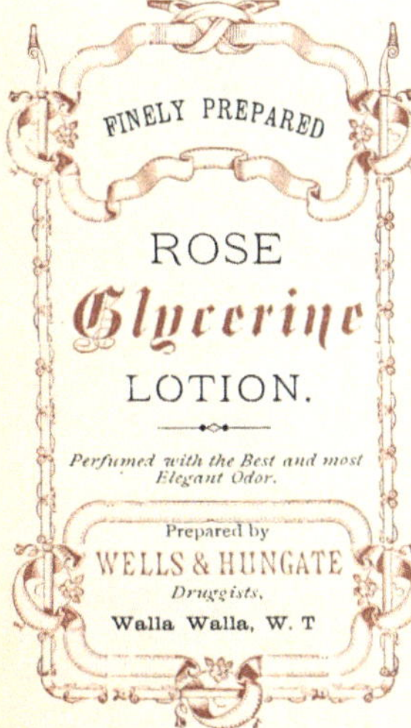

No. 4132—250, 90c; 500, $1.25; 1000, $1.80.

No. 4133—250, 90c; 500, $1.25; 1000, $1.80.

All Labels shown in Black Ink can be printed in Green, Lake or Brown Ink, for 20 per cent extra, on Tinted Paper for 25 per cent extra, or in two colors for 50 per cent extra, to the cost in Black Ink.

Nos. 4132 and 4133 trimmed close to border without extra charge.

McNeil Bros., San Jose, Cal.

Toilet Labels.

No. 4135.
250, $1.35; 500, $1.90; 1000, $2.75.

No. 4136.
250, $1.10; 500, $1.60; 1000, $2.25.

No. 4137.
250, $1.00; 500, $1.50; 1000, $2.00.

No. 4138—250, $1.25; 500, $1.75; 1000, $2.50.

PLEASE REMEMBER,

This Book remains the property of McNEIL BROS., and is loaned upon condition that it is not to be cut or mutilated in any way. In ordering, give No. of pattern, and then write out any changes that may be desired.

No. 4142.
250, 80c; 500, $1.10; 1000, $1.60.

No. 4139.
250, 70c; 500, 95c; 1000, $1.40.

NOTICE.—No. 4139 can also be furnished in Black, Lake, Green or Brown Ink, at prices corresponding to same size in those colors.

No. 4140.
250, 70c; 500, 95c; 1000, $1.40.

No. 4141.
250, 70c; 500, 95c; 1000, $1.40.

No. 4143.
250, 75c; 500, $1.00; 1000, $1.50.

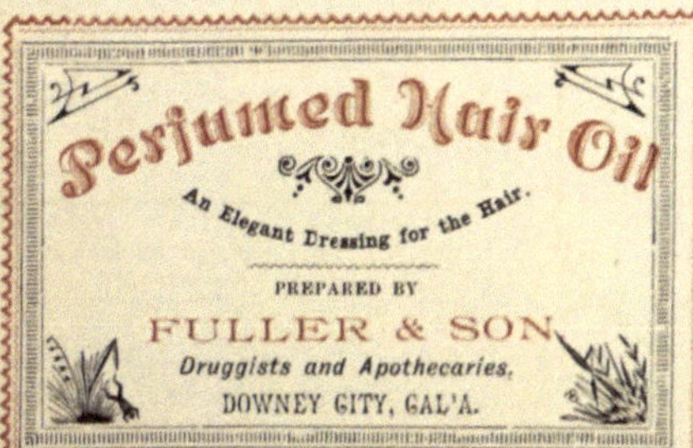

No. 4144.
250, 60c; 500, 85c; 1000, $1.20.

No. 4145.
250, 75c; 500, $1.00; 1000, $1.50.

No. 4146.
250, 70c; 500, 95c; 1000, $1.40.

McNeil Bros., San Jose, Cal.

Bay Rum Labels.

No. 4147—250, $1.25; 500, $1.75; 1000, $2.50.

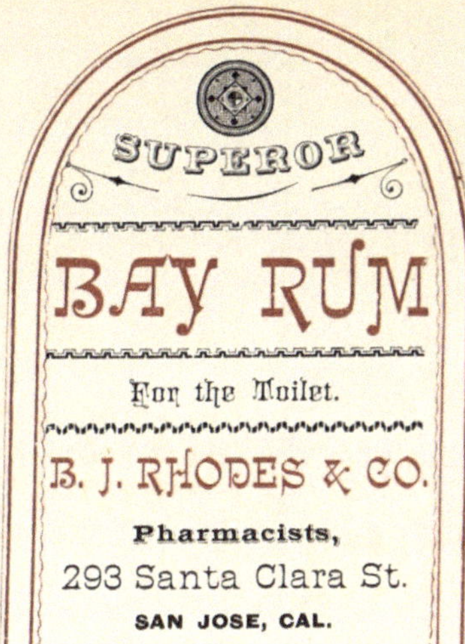

No. 4148—250, $1.10; 500, $1.60; 1000, $2.25.

No. 4149—250, $1.25; 500, $1.75; 1000, $2.50.

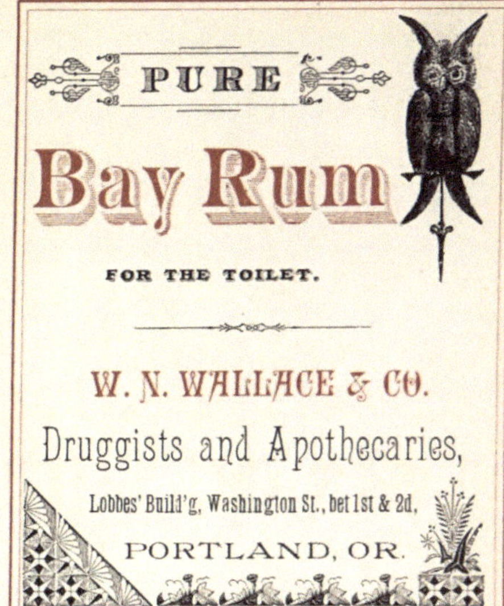

No. 4150—250, $1.10; 500, $1.75; 1000, $2.50.

No. 4151—250, $1.25; 500, $1.75; 1000, $2.50.

No. 4152—250, $1.00; 500, $1.40; 1000, $2.00.

PLEASE OBSERVE.

No. 4152 can also be furnished in Black, Lake, Green or Brown Ink, at prices corresponding to same size in those colors. Always state color of Ink desired.

No. 4153—250, $1.25; 500, $1.75; 1000, $2.50.

No 4154—250, 70c; 500, 95c; 1000, $1.40.

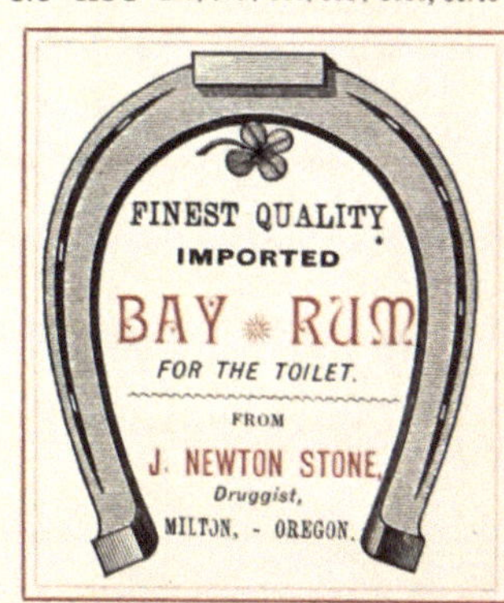

No. 4154 can also be furnished in Black, Lake, Green or Brown Ink, at prices corresponding to same size in those colors.

This Specimen Book is only loaned, and under no circumstances is it to be cut or mutilated in any way. Except through loss by fire, a second copy will not be supplied.

McNeil Bros., San Jose, Cal.

92

Liquor Labels.

No. 4155—250, $1.25; 500, $1.75; 1000, $2.50.

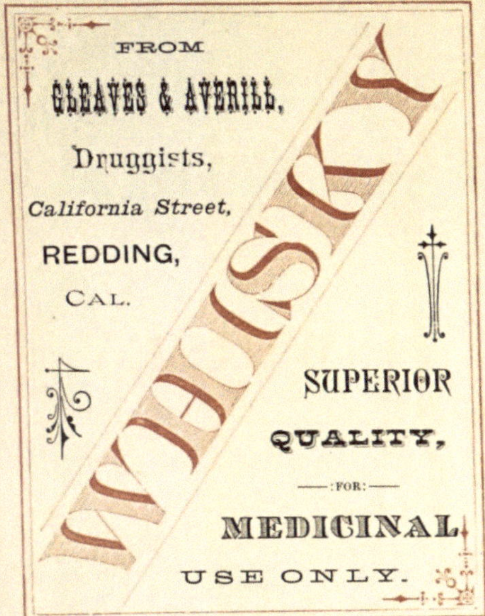

No. 4156—250, $1.25; 500, $1.75; 1000, $2.50.

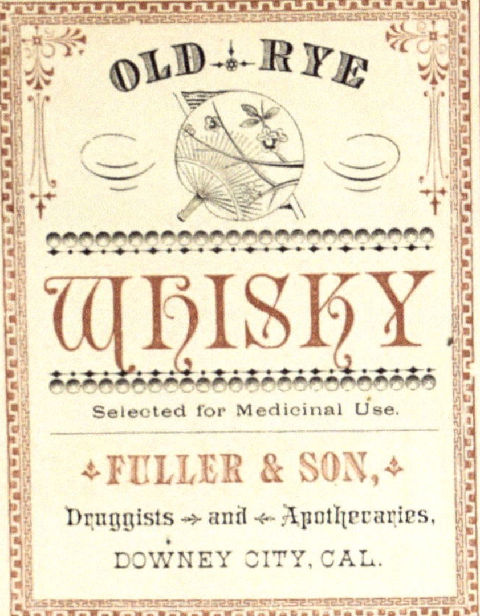

Please remember we do not print less than 250
Labels to any one name of article.

No. 4157—250, $1.35; 500, $1.90; 1000, $2.75.

FINE OLD

SHERRY WINE

FOR MEDICINAL USE.

FROM

CORNER DRUG STORE,

JOE WARNER, - PROPRIETOR,

Elaine Block,

MODESTO,   CALIFORNIA

No. 4158—250, $1.50; 500, $2.00; 1000, $3.00.

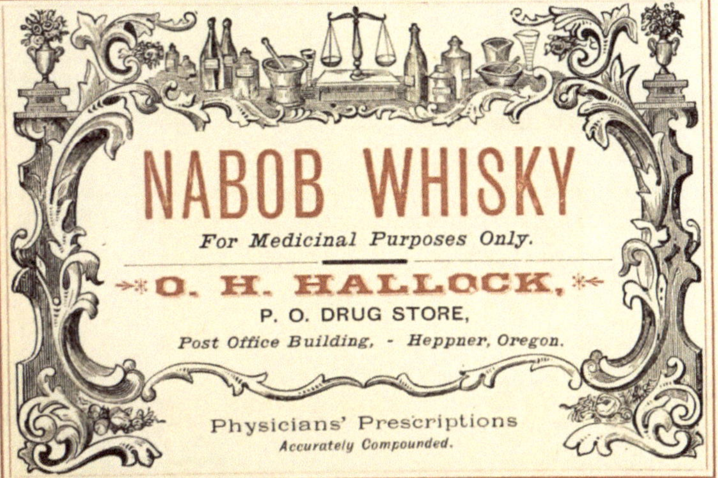

No. 4159—250, $1.10; 500, $1.60; 1000, $2.25.

NEW RUM

For Medicinal Purposes.

FROM

APOTHECARIES' HALL,

B. GUTIERREZ,

SANTA BARBARA, CAL'A.

In all Labels shown on this page the name of
any Wine or Liquor will be inserted
without extra charge.

No. 4160—250, $1.25; 500, $1.75; 1000, $2.50.

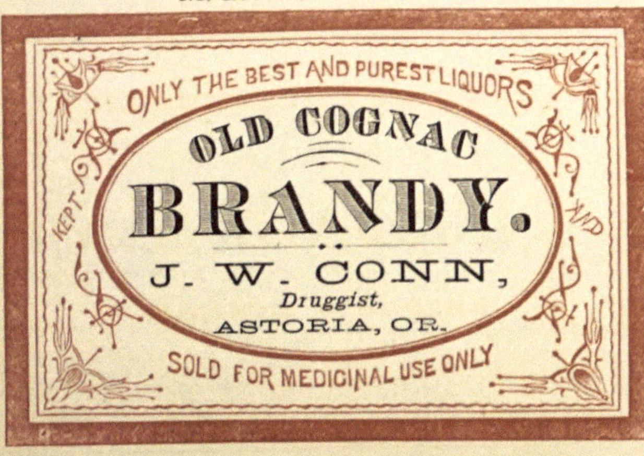

No. 4161—250, $1.25; 500, $1.75; 1000, $2.50.

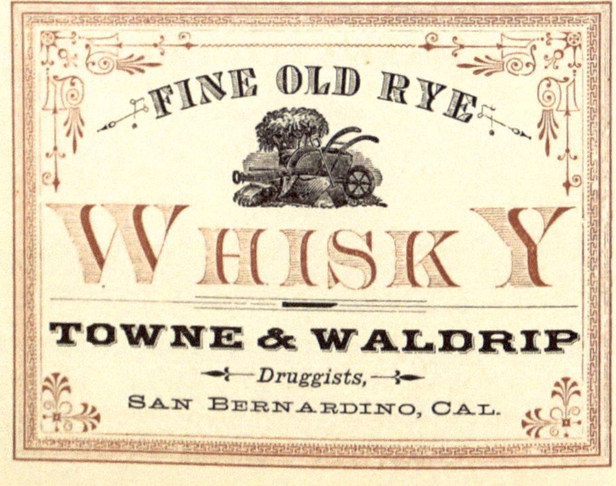

McNeil Bros., San Jose, Cal.

Liquor Labels.

No. 4162—250, $1.75; 500, $2.35; 1000, $3.50.

No. 4163—250, $1.50; 500, $2.00; 1000, $3.00.

No. 4164—250, $1 25; 500, $1.75; 1000, $2.50.

We do not print less than 250
Labels to each name of article.

No. 4166—250, $1.25; 500, $1.75; 1000, $2.50.

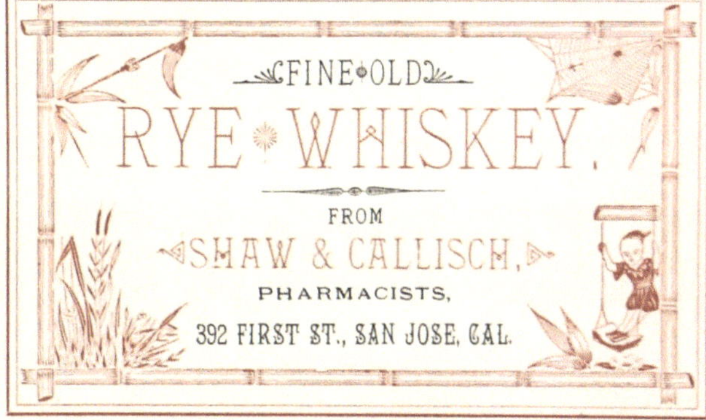

No. 4165—250, $1.50; 500, $2.00; 1000, $3.00.

No. 4167—250, $1 25; 500, $1.75; 1000, $2.50.

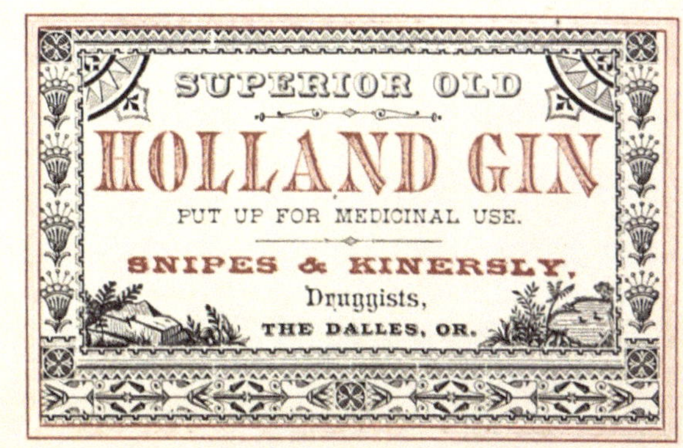

In all Labels shown on this page the name of any
Wine or Liquor will be inserted without extra charge.

We do not print less than 250 Labels to each name
of article, except when expressly so stated on top.

Please **DO NOT** cut or mutilate this Book, but order
by Number of Pattern, and name articles wanted.

McNeil Bros., San Jose, Cal.

No. 4168—250, $1.50; 500, $2.00; 1000, $3.00.

No. 4169—250, $1 25; 500, $1 75; 1000, $2.50.

No. 4172.
250, $1.60; 500, $2.20; 1000, $3.25.

No. 4170—250, $1.10; 500, $1.60; 1000, $2.25.

No. 4171.
250, $1.25; 500, $1.75; 1000, $2.50.

Labels Nos. 4168, 4169, and 4170 are
trimmed close to borders, making dia-
mond shaped Labels when complete.

The name of any Wine or Liquor inserted without extra charge.

McNeil Bros., San Jose, Cal.

READ CAREFULLY BEFORE ORDERING.

Black Ink—No. 3667½.	Two Colors—No. 4180.
250, $1.10; 500, $1.60; 1000, $2.25.	250, $1.35; 500, $1.90; 1000, $2.75.

No. 4181. In Stock—50c per 100. Over 100, Class S. The name of any Wine or Liquor inserted at same rates. We do not furnish less than 100 to a name.

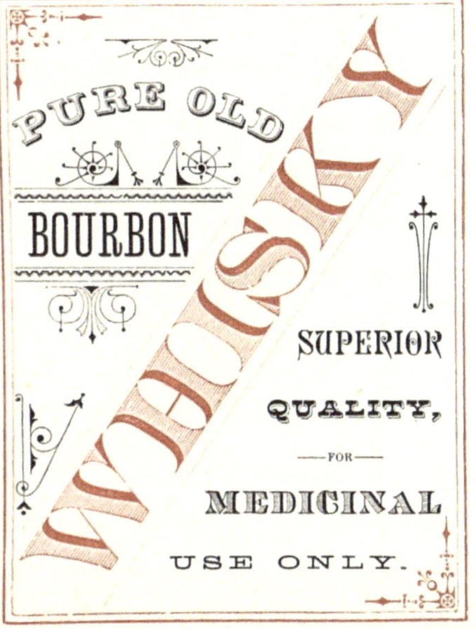

No. 4182. In Stock—50c per 100. Over 100, Class S. The name of any Wine or Liquor inserted.

No. 4183.
250, 70c; 500, 95c; 1000, $1.40.

Attention is called to the above Label, which we have adopted since the first part of this book was printed. It will be found a valuable intermediate size, between Nos. 4163 and 4164, and can be furnished in Black Ink when desired at the price above quoted.

The name of any Wine or Liquor will be inserted, in any Liquor Label, at the prices quoted.

Again we request the Trade not to cut or mutilate this Specimen Book in any way, it having cost us much labor, as well as money. In ordering it is only necessary to give us the Number of the Pattern, and write out the names of articles or changes that are desired.

Except when expressly so stated, on top of each Label, we do no not print less than 250 to each name.

No. 4183 is also a new design, for which we bespeak a pleasing reception by lovers of novelties. It can be furnished in Black, if desired, at the following prices:

250, 60c; 500, 85c; 1000, $1.20.

In ordering the above Label for Black Ink, it will be necessary to so state it, otherwise it will be furnished as above.

Nos. 4184 to 4189—In Stock, at 25c per 100. Over 100, Class I. Any Extract furnished at same rates.

No. 4184.	No. 4185.	No. 4186.	No. 4187.	No. 4188.	No. 4189.

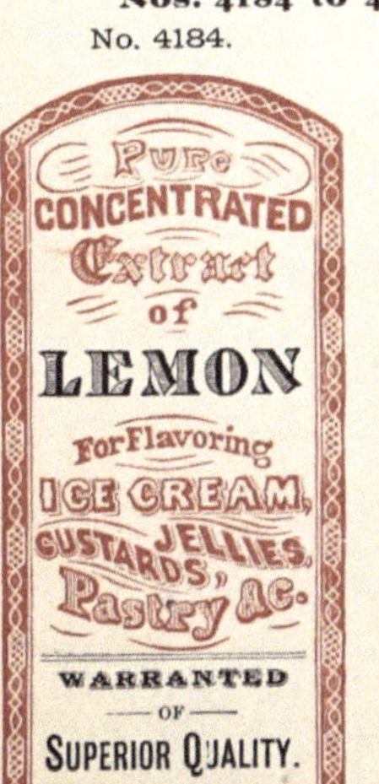

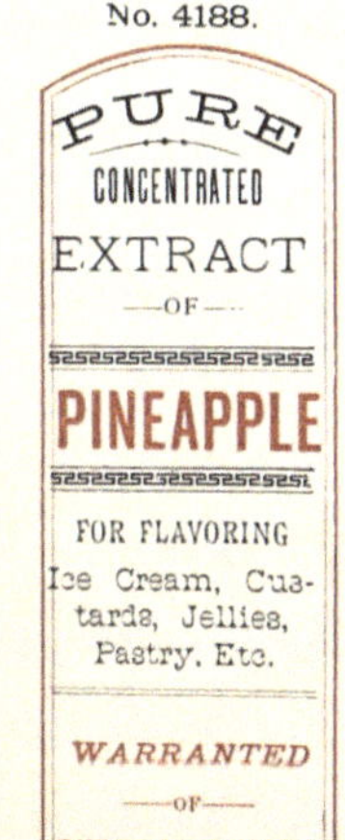

New Elite Series.

In this beautiful Series of Labels the lovers of "Unique" designs have abundant scope in which to indulge their fancies, our very extensive facilities enabling us to furnish almost any shape or style of border that may be wished, in which the most modern faces of type will be used, and the best of workmanship will at all times be employed. This is not intended as a "cheap" Series, and should only be ordered by those who appreciate the advantages of the finer grades of Labels, and who are willing to pay a fair price for the same. Although it is quite impossible to here quote prices for all Labels in this style, we will be pleased to give prices on application, and in general they will run about as here named. These Labels will not be gummed. Order "New Elite Series."

No. 4216—250, 50c; 500, 70c; 1000, $1.00.

MAX CLERICUS,
PACIFIC DRUG STORE,
Cor. Front and Madison Sts., Seattle, W. T.

No......................... Dr.........................
Directions:.........................

No. 4217—250, 65c; 500, 90c; 1000, $1.30.

CITY DRUG STORE,
A. HALIBURTON, Proprietor,
Bridge Street, - REDWOOD CITY, CAL'A.

No......................... Dr.........................
Directions:.........................

No. 4218—250, 90c; 500, $1.25; 1000, $1.80.

→DEL MONTE DRUG STORE,←
J. F. E. HEINTZ, M. D.
MONTEREY. - - CAL'A.

No.........................
Dr.........................
Directions:.........................

The above Labels are furnished by the Series

AT THE FOLLOWING PRICES:

250 of each size,	(750 Labels,)	$ 1.25
500 of each size,	(1500 Labels,)	2.25
1000 of each size,	(3000 Labels,)	3.75
2000 of each size,	(6000 Labels,)	6.50
5000 of each size,	(15000 Labels,)	15.00

These Labels are cut, and are neatly done up in rubber bands ready for use, but they are not gummed (except on white paper.)

We do not print less than 250 Labels to any one name of article.

No. 4219—250, $1.50; 500, $2.00; 1000, $3.00.

SUPERIOR
Eau de Cologne
FOR THE TOILET.
C. A. McDONELL,
Druggist and Chemist,
271 N. MAIN STREET, ROSE BLOCK,
Los Angeles.

No. 4220.
250, $1.25; 500, $1.75; 1000, $2.50.

ROSE
HAIR OIL
—PREPARED BY—
G. A. SPRECHER, M. D.
Colton Pharmacy,
COLTON, CAL.

No. 4221—250, 90c; 500, $1.25; 1000, $1.80.

FINELY
PERFUMED
HAIR
OIL.
FROM
G. F. NIEGE,
Druggist,
PASADENA, CAL'A.

No. 4222—250, $1.25; 500, $1.75; 1000, $2.50.

HIGHLY PERFUMED
HAIR OIL
—PREPARED BY—
SNIPES & KINERSLY,
Wholesale and Retail Druggists,
THE DALLES, OR.

No. 4223—250, 90c; 500, $1.25; 1000, $1.80.

CRYSTAL PALACE
COLOGNE
—PREPARED BY—
G. A. SPRECHER, M. D.
Colton Pharmacy,
COLTON, CAL.

No. 4224—250, 90c; 500, $1.25; 1000, $1.80.

SUPERIOR
EAU DE
COLOGNE
—PREPARED BY—
R. E. COLLINS,
SAN JOSE, CAL.

No. 4225—250, 75c; 500, $1.00; 1000, $1.50.

SUPERIOR FRENCH
TOOTH POWDER
NAVY YARD DISPENSARY,
MARE ISLAND, CAL.